PIANO SOLO

Motion Picture Artwork TM & Copyright © 2018 Disney

ISBN 978-1-5400-4280-4

Visit Hal Leonard Online at
www.halleonard.com

Contact us:
Hal Leonard
7777 West Bluemound Road
Milwaukee, WI 53213
Email: info@halleonard.com

In Europe, contact:
Hal Leonard Europe Limited
Distribution Centre, Newmarket Road
Bury St Edmunds, Suffolk, IP33 3YB
Email: info@halleonardeurope.com

In Australia, contact:
Hal Leonard Australia Pty. Ltd.
4 Lentara Court
Cheltenham, Victoria, 3192 Australia
Email: info@halleonard.com.au

THE NUTCRACKER AND THE
FOUR REALMS

Music by JAMES NEWTON HOWARD

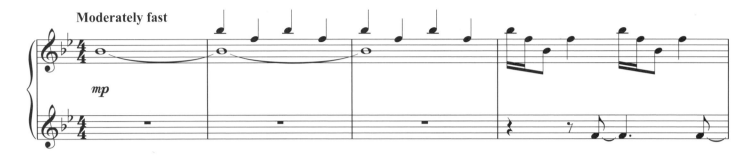

MOUSERINKS

Music by JAMES NEWTON HOWARD

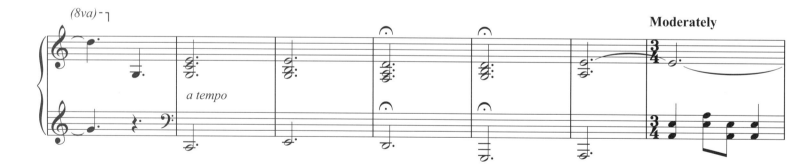

JUST A FEW QUESTIONS

Music by JAMES NEWTON HOWARD

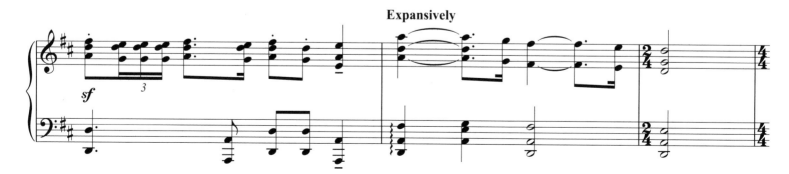

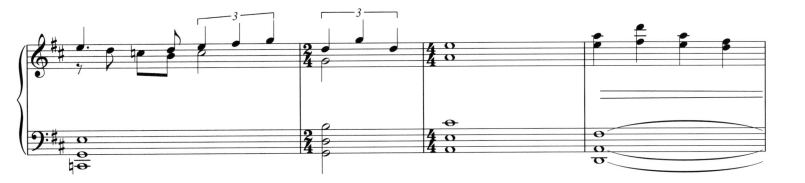

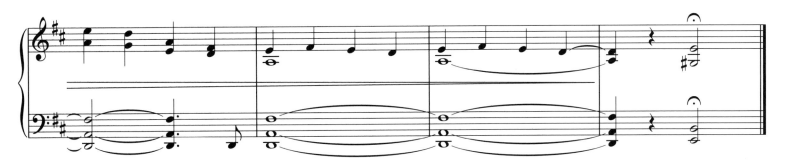

SUGAR PLUM AND CLARA

Music by JAMES NEWTON HOWARD

Moderately, expressively

CLARA FINDS THE KEY

Music by JAMES NEWTON HOWARD

Moderately fast

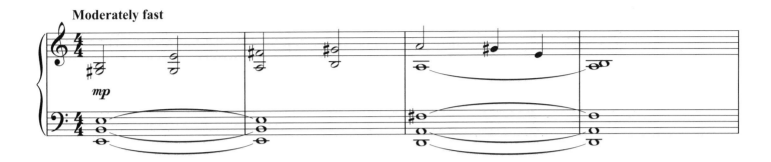

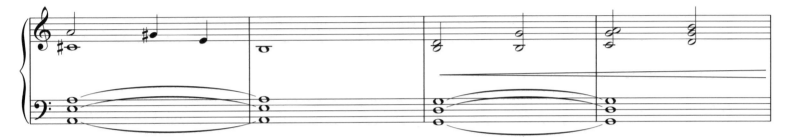

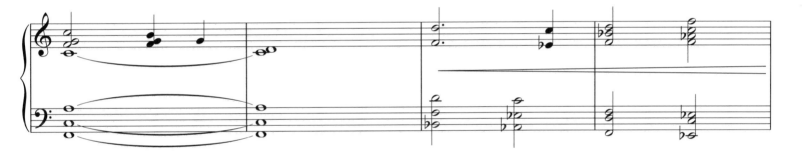

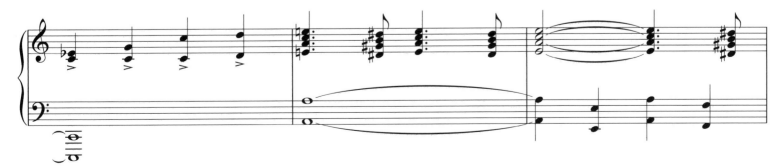

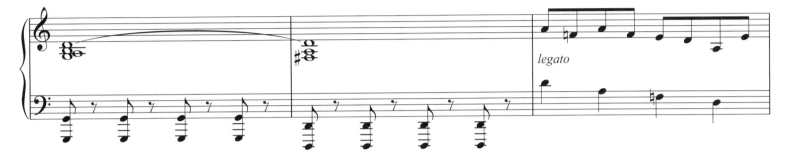

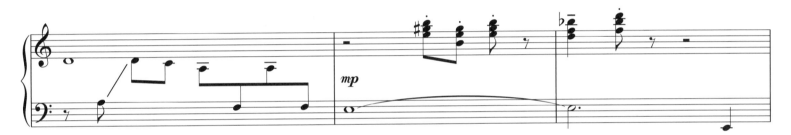

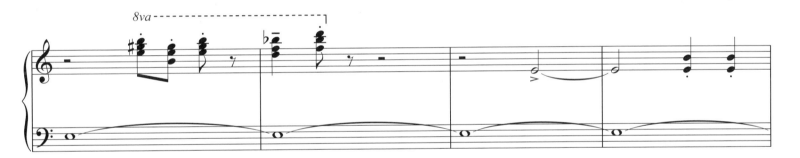

THE MACHINE ROOM FIGHT

Music by JAMES NEWTON HOWARD

Moderately fast

mf

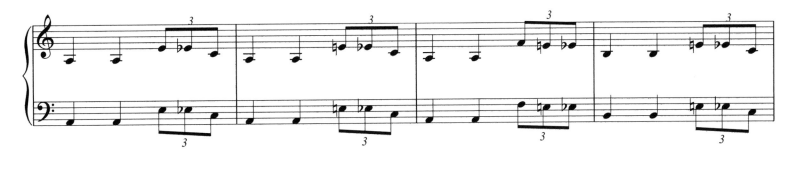

FALL ON ME

Written by IAN AXEL,
CHAD VACCARINO, MATTEO BOCELLI
and FORTUNATO ZAMPAGLIONE

* Recorded a half step lower.

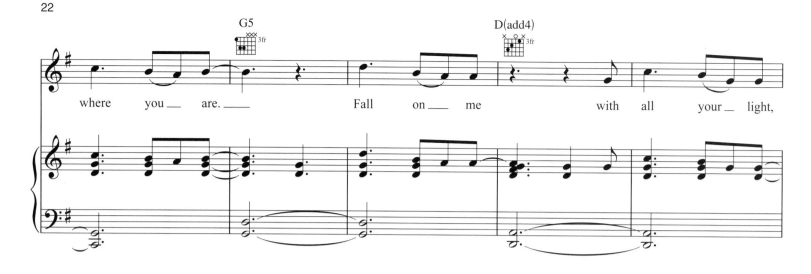

where you __ are. ___ Fall on __ me with all your __ light,

with all _____ your light, with all _____ your light.

Soon you will find what your heart wants to know. Don't give up hope for I

know you are close. __ And all you have ev - er dreamed, wished you could ev - er be is wait - ing to find you where -

ev - er you go. ___ Be - lieve in your-self ev'ry step that you take, ___ know I am smil - ing with

pride ev - 'ry day. My love will for-ev - er be strong-er than stone. Don't be a-fraid, you are

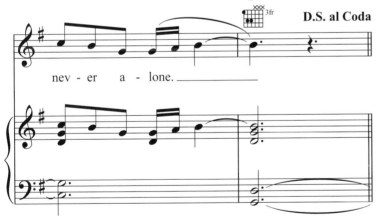

nev - er a - lone. ___

D.S. al Coda

CODA

___ your light. ___

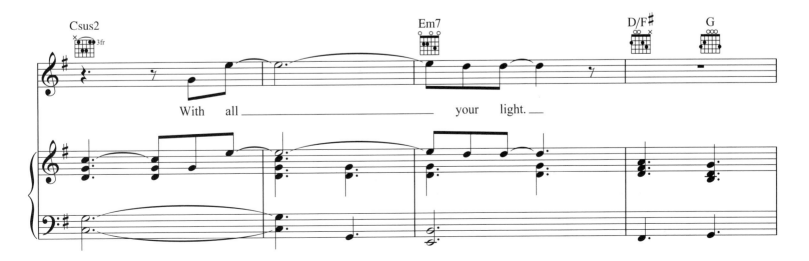

With all ___ your light. ___

ab - brac - cia - mi. ___ Fall on ___ me, ___ with

all your ___ light, with all _____ your light, with all ___

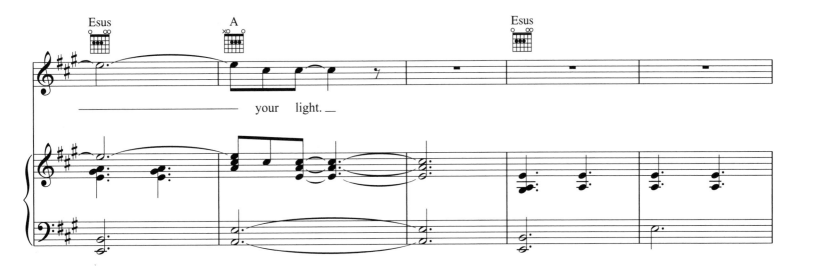

_____ your light. ___

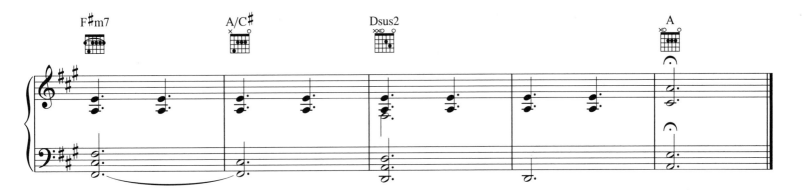

THE NUTCRACKER SUITE

Music by JAMES NEWTON HOWARD

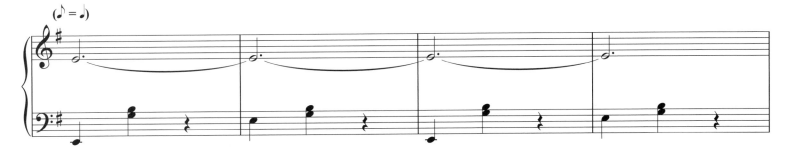

Freely

(♩. = ♪)